Defense in Depth: An Impractical Strategy For a Cyber World

Prescott E. Small

November, 2011

Businesses and Information Technology Security Professionals have spent a tremendous amount of time, money and resources to deploy a Defense in Depth approach to Information Technology Security. Yet successful attacks against RSA, HB Gary, Booz, Allen & Hamilton, the United States Military, and many others are examples of how Defense in Depth, as practiced, is unsustainable and the examples show that the enemy cannot be eliminated permanently. A closer look at how Defense in Depth evolved and how it was made to fit within Information Technology is important to help better understand the trends seen today. Knowing that Defense in Depth, as practiced, actually renders the organization more vulnerable is vital to understanding that there must be a shift in attitudes and thinking to better address the risks faced in a more effective manner. Based on examples in this paper, a change is proposed in the current security and risk management models from the Defense in Depth model to Sustained Cyber-Siege Defense. The implications for this are significant in that there have to be transitions in thinking as well as how People, Process and Technology are implemented to better defend against a never ending siege by a limitless number and variety of attackers that cannot be eliminated. The suggestions proposed are not a drastic change in operations as much as how defenses area aligned, achieve vendor collaboration by applying market pressures and openly sharing information with each other as well as with federal and state agencies. By more accurately describing the problems, corporations and IT Security Professionals will be better equipped to address the challenges faced together.

1. Defense in Depth: A Flawed strategy for a Sustained Cyber-Siege:

Defense in Depth was developed to defend a kinetic or real world military or strategic assets by creating layers of defense that compel the attacker to expend a large amount of resources, while straining supply lines. The tactical goal is to delay and render the enemy attack unsustainable. This strategy results in leaving the attacker vulnerable for counter attack. The defender is then able to counter attack the enemy and eliminate the threat.

In the kinetic world, Loss of Strength Gradient (LSG) is a key indicator of the effectiveness of Defense in Depth. The LSG demonstrates that the further away the attacker is from the target of aggression the less strength that could be made available. (Wikipedia, 1962) The evidence has shown that geographic distance is irrelevant to Cyber-Defense. Attackers can be on the opposite side of the planet and be as effective as someone sitting in the parking lot. In fact, the evidence shows that the opposite of LSG is true for attackers residing outside the borders of the United States. Many attackers are immune to a response by law enforcement because of the restrictions of international borders and the lack of laws being enforced or even existing to stop such activity.

Defense in Depth, in its original concept, works for a kinetic world defense. The problem with Defense in Depth in the world of Cyber-Defense is that it is unsustainable. Practitioners of Information

Prescott E. Small

Technology Security exercise a component of Defense in Depth called a "Layered Defense". What Defense in Depth is and what security practitioner's do are not the same because the Layers of Defense is only a component of the Defense in Depth strategy. While the Defense in Depth strategy requires this element, having Layered Defenses alone does not fulfill the requirements of Defense in Depth as a whole.

What is practiced in the civilian sectors cannot be called Defense in Depth because the civilian sector can never fulfill the original intent of the strategy and counter attack to destroy the enemy.

For one, a Counter-attack would not be legal and secondly the ethics of a counter attack would be questionable at best. Thirdly, at the minimum, counter attacking would not be cost effective or practical for those practicing Cyber-Defense with their existing challenges and strained resources. A counter attack from the public sector would not have a return on investment, would likely result in escalation of the attack and increase costs with little to no measurable benefit for the effort. For evidence of this opinion one need only take a look at the reactions from groups like Anonymous and their attacks against HB Gary or PayPal. There is no profit in provocation. (Associated Press, 2011; Goodin, 2011; Lennon, 2011; McMillan, 2011)

To be fair it needs to be pointed out that the Defense in Depth concept has been co-opted by many different industries and no longer resembles the original strategy for the kinetic world of the military. While this paper is focused on the application of Defense in Depth in Information Security there are many other applications that demonstrate the dilution of the original concept.

Some additional adaptations of Defense in Depth include the following:

- Fire Prevention – "…requires the deployment of fire alarms, extinguishers, evacuation plans, mobile rescue and fire-fighting equipment" (The Australian, 2011)

- Nuclear Energy – "denotes the practice of having multiple, redundant, and independent layers of safety systems for the single, critical point of failure: the reactor core." (Wikipedia, 2011)

- Engineering – "…emphasizes redundancy - a system that keeps working when a component fails - over attempts to design components that will not fail in the first place." (Wikipedia, 2011)

- Online Gaming – In Xbox Live Battlefield 2 "The objective of the defense in depth is to defeat the attacker by attrition, trading ground for kill/tickets." (Phalanx, 2011)

Practitioners of Cyber-Security are constantly force fed, by vendors, trainers, books and articles that Defense in Depth is the only and best strategy to protect their most valuable assets. Practitioners are also being told that Defense in Depth works.

The evidence shows that Defense in Depth has been turned against IT Security Departments and is now a strategy that the attackers are depending on to provide them the opportunities they require to facilitate a successful attack.

As a result of Defense in Depth implementations individuals, corporations, and government entities are being made victims of an attack strategy that is really more akin to Defense in Depth in reverse. The attackers provoke the maintenance of a layered defensive stance that is massive, difficult to manage, requires extensive skill sets and is extremely costly. In essence, the attackers are forcing an unsustainable posture, exhausting resources and adapting advanced persistent and advanced evasive techniques to slip right past People, Process and Technology.

No matter what actions are taken and what tools are used, even if an attacker is ejected, that attacker is simply siting at the perimeter trying new strategies. Unless the attacker is somehow permanently removed from the threat scape, then the threat posed by an attacker is only temporarily mitigated. Considering the supply of attackers in the world, the evidence shows how the attack model has really evolved into a Sustained Cyber-Siege.

Prescott E. Small

We can see the failings of Defense in Depth in the attacks that recently made headlines:

- Sony – Partial loss of $ 343,750,000 for 1 month of lost services alone. There are currently 55 Lawsuits so far in the U.S. as well as the damage to reputation and brand. (Peckham, 2011)

- RSA – According to a report in The Washington Post, the cost of the RSA hack which compromised the security of RSA's SecurID products was $66 million. (Tsukayama, 2011)

- IMF – The New York Times recently reported "highly confidential information about the fiscal condition of many nations" contain "political dynamite" that could affect global markets…" (Paul, 2011)

- Epsilon – "…Epsilon hack may be the largest name and email address breach in the history of the Internet." (Storm, 2011)

- Citigroup – "Citigroup has been forced to reveal that a recent hack of its network exposed the financial data of more than 360,000 customers" (Zetter, 2011)

- ManTech – "…the members (Anonymous) posted a 390 MB download that appeared to contain reports related to NATO, the US Army and personnel files." (Lennon, 2011)

- U.S. Military's Predator Drones – the response to the persistent key logger on the armed drones was "We keep wiping it off, and it keeps coming back," a source told the technology

magazine. "We think it's benign. But we just don't know."
(The Australian, 2011)

- Booz, Allen & Hamilton – "Anonymous hackers boasted of stealing passwords linked to some 90,000 military users, although The Associated Press counted only about 67,000 unique email addresses, of which about 53,000 carried ".mil" domains." (Associated Press, 2011)

The list and the seriousness of the breaches only increases which each press release.

In order for the civilian and business sectors to have success at securing sensitive electronic information and intellectual property then IT Security Professionals must do away with the model known as Defense in Depth and instead adopt a new model of Sustained Cyber-Siege Defense.

1.1. Defense in Depth

Understanding that Defense in Depth model requires a look at the history of how the strategy was developed by the military. The name Defense in Depth is much newer; the strategy itself has been around for millennia. The earliest recorded historical event that can be attributed to such a strategy was first used by Hannibal (Anonymous, 2009) in the Battle of Cannae in the summer of 216 BC during the Second Punic war.

History contains many more examples of the Defense in Depth Strategy:

- American Revolution – "At Springfield, Greene used the same defense in depth approach that later served him well in the South at places like Guilford Court House." (Hickman, n.d.)
- Battle of Gettysburg – "…the initial defense of Gettysburg is called a "defense in depth". (Whittenburg, 2002)
- World War I – The Germans …"were also the first (In WWI) to apply the concept of "defense in depth," where the front-line zone was hundreds of yards deep and contained a series of redoubts rather than a continuous trench." (Wikipedia, n.d.)
- Iran-Iraq War – "…saw the ultimate development of Iraq's military abilities in the fields of Defense-in-depth and counter offensive operations." (Knights, 2005)

1.1.1. Cyber World versus Kinetic World

Defense in Depth works well for the kinetic world because the rules of the physical world apply and a person cannot simply walk through a solid barrier. In the cyber-world nothing is real; it is all a sea of 1's and 0's performing tasks on real world hardware. The Cyber-World has rules in place but those rules aren't laws that are demonstrated in the physical world; that is what is exploited. The Cyber-World is rife with anomalies, bugs, gaps and holes that allow an attacker to disguise traffic or even make the traffic invisible; simply passing straight through People, Process and Technology. In the Cyber-World activities and actions can be taken that in the kinetic world would be physically impossible. After all, a soldier could not render himself invisible and walk through a wall of fire, yet.

Prescott E. Small

2. Significant Failures in Defense in Depth:

Highlighting the significant failures provides the evidence for this position. One need only to look at the evidence of success in the attacker's efforts to see their labor is bearing fruit:

- The value associated with the attacker's successes is increasing.
- The frequency of successful attacks is increasing.
- The effort required to succeed is decreasing.
- The skill level required to succeed in an attack is decreasing.

Considering the decades of implementation of Defense in Depth in Information Security and how the "strategy" has evolved in Information Technology the evidence should show a steady decrease in the number of successful attacks around the globe as Defense in Depth matures. The simple fact is that even though "Defense in Depth" is the predominant practice those successful attacks are increasing. The ability to stop all network penetrations is essentially impossible. No matter what actions are taken an attacker will penetrate every network at some point.

Some of the thought leaders in Information Security are just starting to come to similar conclusions as well. The Special Cyber Operations Research and Engineering or SCORE Committee (SCORE, 2011) has commissioned the Assumption Buster Workshop to examine if

"Defense-in-Depth Is A Smart Investment for Cyber Security." The National Science Foundation is sponsoring this project early in 2011. They point out that Defense in Depth was *"Initially developed by the military for perimeter protection, Defense-in-Depth was adopted by the National Security Agency (NSA) for main-frame computer system protection."* (SCORE, 2011)

The SCORE committee is seeing the failings in Defense in Depth as well and this is reflected in their stated goal that *"we need to determine how the cyber security community developed confidence in Defense-in-Depth despite mounting evidence of its limitations, and second, we must look at the mechanisms in place to evaluate the cost/benefit of implementing Defense-in-Depth that layers mechanisms of uncertain effectiveness."* (SCORE, 2011)

As the SCORE Committee has pointed out that *"Continuing research that achieves only incremental improvements is a losing proposition. We are lagging behind and need technological leaps to get, and keep, ahead of adversaries who are themselves rapidly improving attack technology. To answer this call, we must examine the key assumptions that underlie current security architectures. Challenging those assumptions both opens up the possibilities for novel solutions that are rooted in a fundamentally different understanding of the problem and provides an even stronger basis for moving forward..."* (SCORE, 2011)

Defense in Depth as it is practiced is not working. The reason for this is that IT Security Professionals do not practice actual Defense in Depth.

3. The NSA Definition of Defense in Depth follows:

Defense in Depth is a practical strategy for achieving Information Assurance in today's highly networked environments. It is a "best practices" strategy in that it relies on the intelligent application of techniques and technologies that exist today. The strategy recommends a balance between the protection capability and cost, performance, and operational considerations. (SCORE, 2011)

Following this explanation and definition it should be obvious that Information Technology Security and Cyber-Defense is not making use of Defense in Depth as a strategy, but rather in name only. Even the NSA's description does not come close to the original descriptions of Defense in Depth. (NSA, n.d.) IT Security Professionals are failing Defense in Depth because IT Security Professionals cannot eliminate the base threat, the enemy. IT Security Professionals are mitigating individual vectors against a near infinite supply of attackers with near infinite resources. Yet IT Security Professionals are faced with defending their environments with limited People, Process and Technology; though some would argue that there is an excess of process.

Prescott E. Small

3.1.1. Defense in Depth; is it failing us?

No, IT Security Professionals are failing Defense in Depth with their inability to complete the mission. As previously stated, there are multiple elements to such a strategy, such as eliminating the enemy, would be impossible and illegal for most. The burden of proof for the failures within Defense in Depth lies with the evidence of the successful attacks that have been so widely publicized. The evidence shows that these attackers have been successful in stealing pretty much whatever they want when it comes to sensitive electronic information and intellectual property resulting in damages that the government, corporations and IT Security Professionals cannot accurately measure. (Associated Press, 2011; Goodin, 2011; Lennon, 2011; McMillan, 2011; Peckham, 2011; Storm, 2011; Tsukayama, 2011; Zetter, 2011)

Many could easily argue that:

"No, it is improper deployments."

"No, the wrong tools were used."

"No, inadequate training was provided."

"No, people weren't reviewing the right logs."

"No, (fill in the blank)."

3.1.2. The truth is two-fold here:

One or all of these and other statements are actually true to some degree. These reasons are likely contributing factors and could easily be attributable to a root cause of an exploited vulnerability. The evidence

Prescott E. Small

shows that the Defense in Depth model is partially responsible. History shows that, at the time, security was neither a concern nor an issue to DARPA and the other participants who invented the internet. It was only later that security protocols and procedures were ad-hoc bolted onto TCP/IP. Then again, later when these practices were found wanting, a more strategic initiative was needed. It was only natural for the Military and Government agencies to adopt what they already knew and understood then adapted the strategy to the then infant version of the internet. The result created the environment that applied the pressures required for the applied strategy to devolve to a function of Defense in Depth; one of layered defenses based on People, Process and Technology. One result of this strategy is a false sense of security that is provided by having compliance with a strategy that cannot be 100% successful. Defense in Depth was adopted as the strategy long before the current risks were understood.

The attackers of today are well versed in the strategies, the technologies and the business practices that are used to define Defense in Depth as IT Security Professionals practice it today. The attackers that IT Security Professionals face have access to the same tools, strategies and best practices that IT Security Professionals have implemented. This also creates opportunity for profitable ventures of testing the malicious software resulting in the attackers improving their strategies and honing their skills. This also provides the groundwork for updating the counter measures aimed at defeating their People, Process and Technology.

These combined elements give the attackers the advantage. "Intrusions into DoD and other information systems over the past decade provide ample evidence that Defense-in-Depth provides no significant barrier to sophisticated, motivated, and determined adversaries given those adversaries can structure their attacks to pass through all the layers of defensive measures." (SCORE, 2011)

A symptom of the unsustainability of Defense in Depth is how the strategy is described as a layered defense commonly compared to an onion. This approach and that description combined with the business practices and standards like ISO, COBIT or ITIL have resulted in creating silos that are no longer actually connected but rather handled like the baton in a rally race. This creates an opportunity for attackers to fly under the radar and establish persistence in a network. This can occur because a narrowed scope can also result in a limiting view of activities. This lack of a seeing the big picture and understanding lots of different yet related events can result in missed detections giving the advantage to the attacker.

IT Security Professionals need to adapt defense strategies to account for the more accurate description of the problem. Information Security needs to be looked at in a more organic fashion through the eyes of Sustained Cyber-Siege Defense.

4. Human Behavior; The Bane of IT Security:

Factors of security are tightly related to how people behave in a given situation. IT Security Professionals and their leadership cannot afford to think in purely strategic and tactical terms without considering what normal human behavior is.

Human behavior, or Layer 8 of the OSI model, or the iD10T error, or "the problem is obviously between the chair and the keyboard" type humor not only highlights the frustrations but also the greatest and most difficult to control vulnerability, the human mind. The attackers must view the human mind as their greatest asset in infiltrating private networks. The evidence lies in the volume of global SPAM rates of close to 1 billion SPAM e-mails per week. (Cisco, 2011) The attackers aren't wasting their time on techniques and tools that don't work.

Risk deferral is a natural part of the human psyche, and one that is not addressed by the strategy of Defense in Depth. The human is also the greatest weakness in those defensive layers. Human nature enables attackers to use social engineering and tempt people with irresistible bait that dupes the end user into being an unwilling participant in their illicit activities.

The same instincts and thought patterns that help humans to avoid being eaten by a lion or avoid an injury from a falling object do people no good in the cyber world. Humans live "...in a world where risks are presented in parts-per-billion statistics or as clicks on a Geiger counter, our amygdala is out of its depth." (Daley, 2011) The way human brains work is just incompatible with the Cyber-World and the risks found in cyber-space. "People are likely to react with little fear to certain types of objectively dangerous risk that evolution has not prepared them for, such as guns, hamburgers, automobiles, smoking and unsafe sex, even when they recognize the threat at a cognition level." as shown by Carnegie Mellon University Researcher George Loewenstein. (Daley, 2011)

I believe the same analysis is relevant to Cyber-Security and the challenges IT Security Professionals face. Unless a person has been exhaustively trained as IT Security Professionals have been then they will not have that aversion to the risky behavior in cyber-space. It is this lack of cognitive recognition and risk deferral that makes an individual vulnerable and susceptible to the social engineering and other attack vectors that are so successful.

5. Sustained Cyber-Siege Defense:

Now that the problem is outlined, how do IT Security Professionals improve?

There is one simple fact IT Security Professionals and their leadership has to consider. There is no "magic bullet" to protect private networks from attackers. No one vendor, product or service can protect any environment from every attacker over a period of time. The best IT Security Professionals can hope for is products and services that are highly effective, and then have overlapping technologies, or Defense in Breadth, that complement one another. The idea being that what is missed with one product is caught by another.

Just remember that Defense in Breadth is still not 100% effective. Attackers will get through regardless of the efforts taken. The best efforts can only keep the intrusions to a minimum. IT Security Professionals need to focus more on preventing the attacker from getting back out to the internet with sensitive electronic information and intellectual property by using overlapping technologies that prevent any data from reaching unauthorized external destinations

One of the primary elements of Sustained Cyber-Siege Defense is establishing multi-vendor approaches to People, Process and Technology. As consumers of the services and technology IT Security Professionals and their leadership have to place market pressures on vendors that compel the suppliers to understand and adopt the multi-vendor approach to the problems. The practice of vendors continuously attempting to replace competitor's technology is doing nothing but hurting the consumers and giving the advantage to the attackers. The only reason a technology should be replaced is if it is ineffective, obsolete or no longer supported.

Another primary element of advancing Sustained Cyber-Siege Defense is *"Defense in Breadth"* (Kewley & Lowry, 2004). As pointed out in the document "Observations of the effects of defense in depth on adversary behavior in cyber warfare" the SCORE committees observations *"lead us to conclude that defense in breadth is equally important as defense in depth."*(Kewley & Lowry, 2004) They identified that an *"important conclusion of this experiment is that defense in depth without defense in breadth can be ineffective for a sophisticated adversary."* (Kewley & Lowry, 2004) It is also important to highlight that they also referred to Defense in Depth as the *"...concept of layered defense is not new in the information assurance arena"* (Kewley & Lowry, 2004) The definition the researchers came up with is that *"Defense in breadth can be defined as multiple mechanisms across multiple attack classes."* (Kewley & Lowry, 2004)

5.1. Profit Motive:

Attackers are also profit driven. Like most businesses the attackers have similar limitations based on cost, the attackers just measure cost differently. If an attack is not profitable to an attacker they are not going to pursue a target for long. Now profit can be measured in many ways other than money. Some profit by recognition of peers, others profit be a sense of patriotic duty and accomplishment while others are focused on actual money for profit motive. Whatever the motivation, the reward they seek is the profit they desire. The goal should be to drive up cost and lower the attacker's profits to a level of unsustainability. IT
Prescott E. Small

Security Professionals can accomplish this by increasing the complexity of the attack through the Sustained Cyber-Siege Defense strategy.

5.2. Actions for Improvement:

These problems are not addressable by a few individuals. This shift in strategy will take a large number of IT Security Professionals to address together. IT Security Professionals have to work towards altering their strategy, create demand for and influence the market to get the change that is required to be successful. The change will take years to achieve, will require rapid adaptation and will require a significant commitment by IT Security professionals and their employers along with federal and state agencies to drive the change that is required in the People, Process and Technology.

IT Security professionals must also place pressure on government agencies to modify regulations to support industries and drive the changes that are required in an intelligent and measurable fashion.

For Example:
1. Sponsor more independent committees and groups along the lines of the SCORE committee.
    a. Sponsors can be:
        i. The Business Sector.
        ii. Not for Profits like Infragard or ISSA.
        iii. Federal and State Governments.

      iv. A combination of any of the above.

2. The private sector must work with Security Vendors to develop collaboration and federal agencies should consider tax incentives for companies to motivate cooperation with competitors.

3. Work with Business and Suppliers to define realistic and enabling policies for federal and state regulation.

4. Invest in research that helps develop new Prevent, Contain and Eradicate technologies. IT Security Professionals especially need development in eradicate capabilities that can eliminate the need to re-image so many systems; especially systems in remote locations with limited bandwidth and resources.

5. Create tax incentives for American Companies that are willing to rapidly adopt these strategies and invest in multiple overlapping defenses for areas deemed important and critical to the U.S. Infrastructure in defense, energy, finance, healthcare and communications.

The primary solution is for Information Technology Security Professionals to start talking and questioning the Status Quo and driving change by creating market pressures with vendors and service providers.

Another component of change is to adopt a vertical market based approach that defines the strategy based on business needs for a particular sector such as Health Care, Oil & Gas, Critical Infrastructure, etc. The need here is simply defined by the similarity of function and business processes.

In addition to a vertical market based strategy IT Security Professionals must also develop methods for cooperation, knowledge sharing and alignment of strategies between competitors and customers in the same market space that does not compromise secrets or competitive data to other companies. IT Security Professionals and their organizations need to be able to share sanitized information about attacks and trends they see so that their competitors and customers can also benefit, thereby protecting the vertical markets.

The attackers are exceptionally good at sharing attack data and selling data that allows more attackers to gain access to sensitive electronic information and intellectual property. Therefore IT Security Professionals and corporations can only benefit by doing the same in sharing attack related information that will allow vertical markets to improve security as a whole while increasing the complexity and costs for the attackers seeking to infiltrate the business.

Cooperation with Federal Authorities and the U.S. Government is also essential. The government only knows about what they find and what they are told about. The FBI and the Federal government can only report on and plan for what they know. Therefore it is in everyone's best interest and the interest of everyone to share attack data with federal and state agencies. Then everyone can expect more from the government in terms of resources and political pressures on bad actors. Without data the government agencies are unable to accurately measure the cost and damages that are occurring. As a business and a member of the community at large there is also a civic duty that companies and individuals should consider when making arguments against sharing. If IT Security Professionals and corporations cannot find a way to share sanitized information then it is unreasonable to expect the authorities to be as effective as they could be.

Vertical Market specific strategies need to have specific goals in mind in order to achieve improved security across the board.

1. IT Security Professionals and corporations must learn to live in a persistent state of Sustained Cyber-Siege and manage risks as continuous and evolving.
2. Expect every prevent technology to be circumvented and plan for how to adapt when the breach does happen.
3. IT Security Professionals must also define the attributes for success with Sustained Cyber-Siege Defense, and change how the business is done in the Information Technology Security world.
4. Define how Defense in Breadth can be achieved to prepare for Sustained Cyber-Siege Defense.

5. Make it more difficult to get data back out of a network than it is to get into a network. Stopping infiltration is impossible; managing data exfiltration across the wire is more likely to succeed.

6. Manage the attacker:

    a. Understand the mindset and motivations driving the attackers.

    b. Feed the attackers false information via honeypots with falsified data.

    c. Increase the attacker's levels of effort.

    d. Drive up the attacker's costs, combine defensive technologies to increase complexity.

    e. Deprive the attackers of the profits and rewards they seek.

    f. Damaging the attacker's reputation is a bonus.

7. Pressure vendors to develop vertical market expertise within their own organizations.

6. Keystones of Sustained Cyber-Siege Defense:

1. Abundant participation - The greater the number of participants then the more effective participants will be in their strategies for Prevent, Detect, Contain and Eradicate. As a result, the metrics should show a reduction in detection times and reduce the amount of time it takes to push attackers out.

2. Rapid and sanitized information sharing.

    a. Vertical Markets must share the data

        i. Strip out company specifics, but share the data. In order for there to be success it is critical for IT Security Professionals to not only have accurate, actionable data, they must get it in a timely fashion as well.

    b. Vendor sharing of sanitized data, even amongst competitors, is also essential to success. Vendors have to cooperate and share sanitized and standardized data to detect and eradicate the attackers. Vendors must develop a standard to share data in a format that is able to be correlated.

        i. All Malware should be identified by hash values and not the dozens of text based aliases seen today.

3. Vendor Relations – many competitors often use the same vendors.

    a. Use market pressures on vendors, even those that compete with one another to deliver required services in a collaborative manner.

    b. Place the demand on vendors to work together, with the business and vertical market peers to deliver a higher quality of combined services.

4. Vendor Specialization – Place pressures on vendors to have services and sales engineers that come from vertical markets that get trained up on the business and processes. The better the vendor understands the business and processes then the more valuable that vendor will be in the long term.

5. Knowledge sharing between vendors and the business. Consideration of an employee exchange program would be a highly effective method for knowledge transfer and sharing.

6. Corporate Citizenship – Corporations need to learn to work with local and federal authorities. The lack of information reaching the state and federal level is inhibiting the government's ability to accurately measure and weigh the risks from criminal and state sponsored attackers. IT Security Professionals must openly cooperate with and share information with the authorities so that their representatives have the information they need to apply pressures through law enforcement and political avenues to help reduce the threats. In order to do so the authorities will require accurate information that paints a clear picture of what is happening nationwide to create opportunity, budgets and develop appropriate resources and responses.

Groups like ISSA and Infragard that are currently pursuing some of these ideas, developing processes and establishing new lines of communication. The effort is only in the very beginning stages and will take commitment, time and open communications to develop into a robust and valuable part of the Sustained Cyber-Siege Defense.

7. Conclusion:

The changes that IT Security Professionals, corporations and the Government need to make are not insignificant, but are achievable.

While these recommendations will increase complexity of defense and increase the cost of defense, IT Security Professionals have to evaluate the cost benefit to the value of losses of the assets at risk and plan appropriately for each environment. Vertical markets could combine financial power to subscribe to combined intelligence services to help fund the efforts of vendors to collaborate for everyone's benefit. If IT Security Professionals are to succeed in increasing the cost, effort and complexity of the efforts required by an attacker, then IT Security Professionals and their organizations will have to do the same within the limits of their budgets. One possible solution would be to have not-for-profit groups like ISSA or Infragard act as brokers of sanitized and shared data, managing subscriptions at cost and providing savings for all participants.

The adversary is currently ahead in the escalation of attack versus defense. The attackers are winning. As a result IT Security Professionals must make dramatic shifts in the market place that include putting market pressures on vendors to do things that are not in their own best interests.

Adopting the Sustained Cyber-Siege Defense will require placing pressures on vendors, even competitors, to work together so that IT Security Professionals can achieve Defense in Breadth to better defend against multiple attack classes than they do today.

The challenges are many, the resources are few and the enemy is evolving. It can seem insurmountable at times, but IT Security Professionals currently have the potential to respond as required in an effective fashion within their limits and emerge successful as long as IT Security Professionals can clearly identify and define the problem while sharing information with each other and the government agencies everyone depends on to protect the nation.

8. References

(1) Peckham, M. (2011, July 22). Sony grappling with 55 u.s. lawsuits after psn hack. PC World, Retrieved from
http://www.pcworld.com/article/236330/sony_grappling_with_55_us_la
wsuits_after_psn_hack.html

(2) Peckham, M. (2011, April 27). Sony grappling with 55 u.s. lawsuits after psn hack. PC World, Retrieved from
http://www.pcworld.com/article/226385/sonys_playstation_network_dis
aster_what_happens_next.html

(3) Paul, I. (2011, June 12). Imf hacked; no end in sight to security horror shows. PC WorldPC World, Retrieved from

http://www.pcworld.com/article/230157/imf_hacked_no_end_in_sight_t
o_security_horror_shows.html

(4) Storm, D. (2011, April 4). Epsilon breach: hack of the century?
[Web log message]. Retrieved from
http://blogs.computerworld.com/18079/epsilon_breach_hack_of_the_ce
ntury

(5) Spicer, J. & Aspan, M. (2011, April 3). More customers exposed as
big data breach grows. Reuters, Retrieved from
http://www.reuters.com/article/2011/04/03/us-citi-capitalone-data-
idUSTRE7321PI20110403

(6) RSA won't talk? assume securid is broken. (2011, March 24). The
Register, Retrieved from
http://www.theregister.co.uk/2011/03/24/rsa_securid_news_blackout/

(7) Goodin, D. (2011, June 6). Stolen rsa data used to hack defense
contractor. The Register, Retrieved from
http://www.theregister.co.uk/2011/06/06/lockheed_martin_securid_hack
/

(8) Zetter, K. (2011, June 16). Citi credit card hack bigger than
originally disclosed. Wired, Retrieved from
http://www.wired.com/threatlevel/2011/06/citibank-hacked/

(9) Associated Press (2011, July 11). Anonymous at it again: defense
contractor hacked. CBS News Tech, Retrieved from
http://www.cbsnews.com/stories/2011/07/11/scitech/main20078614.sht
ml

(10) Goodin, D. (2011, July 30). Anonymous hacks US gov contractor,
airs dirty laundry. The Register, Retrieved from
http://www.theregister.co.uk/2011/07/30/anonymous_claims_mantech_
hack/

(11) lennon, M. (2011, July 29). Anonymous hacks mantech, fbi
cybersecurity contractor. Security Week, Retrieved from

http://www.securityweek.com/anonymous-claims-it-hacked-mantech-fbi-cybersecurity-contractor

(12) McMillan, R. (2011, August 1). Anonymous hackers leak documents from security contractor mantech. Tech World, Retrieved from http://news.techworld.com/security/3294530/anonymous-hackers-leak-documents-from-security-contractor-mantech/

(13) Unknown Author. National Security Agency, Information Assurance Solutions Group. (n.d.). Defense in depth Retrieved from http://www.nsa.gov/ia/_files/support/defenseindepth.pdf

(14) Tsukayama, H. (2011, July 26). Cyber attack on rsa cost emc $66 million. Washington Post. Retrieved from http://www.washingtonpost.com/blogs/post-tech/post/cyber-attack-on-rsa-cost-emc-66-million/2011/07/26/gIQA1ceKbI_blog.html

(15) Wikipedia contributors. (1962). Loss of Strength Gradient. Wikipedia, the free encyclopedia. Wikipedia, The Free Encyclopedia. Retrieved from http://en.wikipedia.org/wiki/Loss_of_Strength_Gradient

(16) Anonymous. (2009, November 18). The battle of cannae. Retrieved from http://www.roman-empire.net/army/cannae.html

(17) Wikipedia contributors. (n.d.). Rope-a-dope. Wikipedia, the free encyclopedia. Wikipedia, The Free Encyclopedia. Retrieved from http://en.wikipedia.org/wiki/Rope-a-dope

(18) Collaborative. Information Assurance Directorate, Information Assurance Technical Framework (2002). Information assurance technical framework (3.1) (IATF CD-ROM). Fort Meade, Maryland : National Security Agency Retrieved from https://www.iad.gov/iad/openDoc.cfm?GwNDXLf08OayyzkKziIt+w==

(19) Greenemeier, L. (2011, June 11). Seeking address: why cyber attacks are so difficult to trace back to hackers. Scientific American, Retrieved from http://www.scientificamerican.com/article.cfm?id=tracking-

(20) Daley, J. (2011, August 7). What you don't know can kill you Discover Magazine, 51-88.

(21) Phalanx, L. (2011, July 16). Bfbc2 field manual – defense in depth (update). Retrieved from http://lambdaphalanx.com/2011/07/16/bfbc2-field-manual-defense-in-depth/

(22) Hickman, K. (n.d.). American revolution: battle of springfield. Retrieved from http://militaryhistory.about.com/od/americanrevolution/p/springfield.htm

(23) Whittenburg, E. (2002, February 3). Defense in depth "john buford's first day defense at the battle of gettysburg". Retrieved from • http://www.civilwarhome.com/buforddefense.htm

(24) Wikipedia contributors. (n.d.). Trench Warfare. Wikipedia, the free encyclopedia. Wikipedia, The Free Encyclopedia. Retrieved from http://en.wikipedia.org/wiki/Trench_warfare

(25) Knights, I. (2005). Cradle of conflict, iraq and the birth of modern u.s. military power. Naval Inst Pr.Retrieved from http://books.google.com/books/feeds/volumes?q=1591144442

(26) SCORE. National Coordination Office, Networking and Information (2011). Assumption buster workshop: defense-in-depth is a smart investment for cyber security (NSF - FR20110207_6637)Special Cyber Operations Research and Engineering Committee SCORE. Retrieved from http://www.nitrd.gov/fileupload/files/FR20110207_6637.pdf

(27) Greenemeier, L. (2011, June 13). The fog of cyberwar: what are the rules of engagement?. Scientific American, Retrieved from http://www.scientificamerican.com/article.cfm?id=fog-of-cyber-warfare&page=1

(28) Greenemeier, L. (2011, June 11). Seeking address: why cyber attacks are so difficult to trace back to hackers. Scientific American, Retrieved from
http://www.scientificamerican.com/article.cfm?id=tracking-cyber-hackers

(29) Stewart, C. (2011, June 16). Fireeye: botnet busters. Bussiness Week, Retrieved from
http://www.businessweek.com/magazine/content/11_26/b423407271200 1.htm

(30) Lightning Never Strikes Twice. Mcgraw-hill dictionary of american idioms and phrasal verbs.

(31) Ely, A. (2011, June 17). Tips for implementing two-factor authentication. Dark Reading, Retrieved from
http://www.darkreading.com/authentication/167901072/security/security -management/230800168/tech-insight-tips-for-implementing-two-factor-authentication.html

(32) Stiennon, R. (2010, June 23). The new anatomy of a hack. Retrieved from http://www.intelligentwhitelisting.com/forum/new-anatomy-hack

(33) Cisco. (2011). Global threat report. Cisco 2Q11 , Q(2),

(34) Kewley, D. & Lowry, J. (2004, November 29). Observations on the effects of defense in depth on adversary behavior in cyber warfare. USMA_IEEE02, 18, 1-8. Retrieved from
www.bbn.com/resources/pdf/USMA_IEEE02.pdf

(35) Wikipedia contributors. (2011). Defense in depth. Wikipedia, the free encyclopedia. Wikipedia, The Free Encyclopedia. Retrieved from
http://en.wikipedia.org/wiki/Defence_in_depth

(36) A persistent keylogger virus has infiltrated the us military drone network. (2011, October 10). The Australian. Retrieved from "We keep

wiping it off, and it keeps coming back," a source told the technology magazine. "We think it's benign. But we just don't know."

(37) Fowler, T. (2011, October 13). Cybercrime becomes bigger threat to energy industry than terrorists. FuelFix. Retrieved from http://fuelfix.com/blog/2011/10/13/cybercrime-becomes-bigger-threat-to-energy-industry-than-terrorists/

PRESCOTT E. SMALL
Data Loss Prevention Specialist

As a Data Loss Prevention Specialist I believe it is important to share what I believe my title means in relation to what others might assume it to mean. Data Loss Prevention is a product line for many vendors out there so the title could imply that I am an expert in these products or technologies. I believe that the use of DLP to describe a product line or technology is a bit misleading. I see Data Loss Prevention as the goal of the organization. The products and services we use are oriented to achieve that goal of preventing the loss of tour data. As a Data Loss Prevention Specialist is just a more accurate description of what an IT Security Professional is and what my ultimate goal is in IT Security.

Prescott is an Information Technology and Security Specialist with over 20 years hands-on experience. His resume includes a wide range of technologies beginning with DEC Mainframes and Apple 512K systems along through the entire evolution of the Windows Operating Systems since Windows 3.1. Prescott's current responsibilities focus in IT security, including incident management. He currently holds the GIAC Gold Security Essentials Certification (GSEC). GSEC certification ensures the holder has real-world security awareness in several areas of IT security including computer, network and software.

Prescott began his IT career with his father at Scientific Placement working on the DEC mainframes. After leaving Scientific Placement, he spent the next several years at Telecheck working in the Shared Global Services division, which handled real-time credit card transaction processing and settlements. His job responsibilities included credit fraud control and profiling to prevent credit card fraud as well as assisting authorities with criminal investigations. Prescott then spent two years at Mitsubishi Caterpillar Forklift America (MCFA) operating the desktop support for the Houston offices working for MIT Computers.

Prescott came to Baker Hughes 1998 in the Baker Oil Tools division where he supported field operations for the Eastern United States. After shared services were formed, Prescott went to work in Desktop Support where he was the on-site coordinator at Baker Oil Tools at Navigation Boulevard and Baker Petrolite in Sugar Land.

Prescott transferred to the Windows 2000 Migration Project where he was part of the team that designed and implemented the global transition to windows 2000, Active Directory and developed some of our current IT standards.

Prescott has also worked on several other small and large-scale projects at Baker Hughes during his career.

At the conclusion of the Windows 2000 Migration Project, Prescott transitioned into what is now the IT Tools Team. As a member of the IT Tools Team Prescott was responsible for virus incident management and security related software including the McAfee ePolicy Orchestrator. His responsibilities also included supporting and designing the McAfee products infrastructure. As a result, the IT Tools Team has greatly reduced the number of virus outbreaks ensuring that the corporate network is operational and secure. For the past five years, Prescott has focused almost exclusively on IT Security, Risk Management and Incident Response.

In addition to Prescott's background in IT he is also an accomplished photographer having recently been published.

Prescott's lovely wife Alex is a practicing attorney in the Houston area and they have two wonderful boys, Nicolaus and Zachary.

Prescott attended Houston Community College and the University of Arizona in Tucson. Prescott has held several IT related certifications over the years now has a SANS affiliated GIAC Gold Security Essentials Certification (GSEC).